Produced by AA Publishing

Captions by Richard Cavendish

Filmset by Wyvern Typesetting Ltd, Bristol
Origination by Scantrans Pte Ltd, Singapore
Printed and bound by New Interlitho SpA, Italy

The contents of this publication are believed correct
at the time of printing. Nevertheless, the publishers
cannot accept responsibility for errors or omissions,
or for changes in details given.

A CIP catalogue record for this book is available
from the British Library.

Published by The Automobile Association, Fanum
House, Basing View, Basingstoke, Hampshire
RG21 2EA.

ISBN 0 7495 0151 0

Front cover: Top – *Mechanical statues in
Southgate Street above bakers*
Main – *Arlington Row, Bibury*
Back cover: *Upper Slaughter in spring*
Title page (opposite): *Cottages in the village of
Stanton*

COTSWOLDS

Visions of Cotswolds conjures up images of warm, honey-coloured stone, rolling uplands and a feeling of peace and well-being. Using photographs selected from the AA's picture library, it reveals the unique character of this delightful region of the English countryside, with its chequerboard of stonewalled fields and its beautiful old cottages, houses and churches — so much a feature of the landscape.

Cotswolds

Below *Painswick is typical of the charming old stone-built small towns and villages of the Cotswolds whose prosperity was founded on the wool trade well down into the late 18th century. Making a bow to wool, one of the houses is now the Little Fleece bookshop.*

Opposite page *St Mary's Church, Painswick, is famous for the yew trees in its churchyard. One tradition says there are 99 of them, another that they can never be counted. Among them is a fine array of table tombs of the 17th and 18th centuries, richly carved with bat-winged skulls, plump cherubs, festoons, scrolls and shells and other emblems. Many were the work of a noted monumental mason named John Bryan, who is buried here himself.*

Right *Old houses near the church. Cotswold stone has been used for building since time out of mind and varies slightly in hue depending on where it was quarried. In the Painswick area the stone has a silvery tinge.*

Cotswolds

Cotswolds

Previous spread *The Cotswold area is famed for its attractive villages, and no less a judge than William Morris thought Bibury 'the most beautiful village in England'. It stands among gentle hills in the valley of the River Coln. In the foreground is a good example of a stout Cotswold drystone wall.*

Right *Hay tossing at Chipping Campden, the most important of the old Cotswold wool towns. Dover's Hill outside the town is the site of the annual Dover's Games, originally started by Robert Dover in 1612 as the Cotswold 'Olympicks'. Events include singlestick, wrestling, bowling, sack races, pony races and the painful pastime of shin kicking.*

Right *Dover's Games are now held on the eve of Scuttlebrook Wake, Chipping Campden's annual May festival, which used to be celebrated at Whitsun, but has now moved to the weekend after the Spring Bank Holiday. The torchlight procession through the town is an unforgettable sight.*

Below *The mayor of Chipping Campden, the town beadle and other dignitaries go in procession to the town square. In the background is the May Queen in her portable bower.*

Left *Morris man in red, green and yellow, on the occasion of Dover's Games. The event became so boisterous and rowdy that it was closed down in the 19th century, but a politer version was revived in 1951.*

Opposite page *The River Stour meanders gently through the flat Warwickshire countryside near Shipston-on-Stour. The river rises in the Cotswold hills to the north of Chipping Norton.*

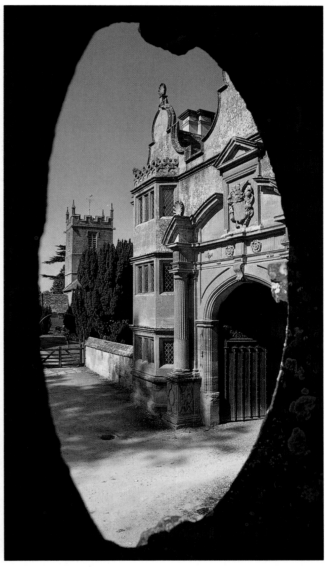

Left *A brightly painted narrowboat has negotiated St John's Lock on the River Thames at Lechlade. In the background is what Shelley described as 'the dim and distant spire' of the church of St Lawrence.*

Above *The rich golden-stone Jacobean gatehouse of Stanway House, between Winchcombe and Broadway in Gloucestershire, glows in the afternoon sunshine. In the background is the church of St Peter.*

Right *Villas, forts and roads survive in the Cotswolds from the period when Britain was the northern-most province of the Roman Empire. The villa at Chedworth, set deep in a sheltered valley north of Cirencester, was rediscovered in 1864.*

Right *This bronze statuette of a priest is one of the finds on display at Chedworth. In one corner of the site there was a shrine to the goddess of the spring which supplied the house with water.*

Right *Coin of Agrippa, in the Corinium Museum at Cirencester. This former Roman town of Corinium was the capital of the local Celtic tribespeople, the Dobunni.*

Left *Detail of a sea creature, from a Roman mosaic in the Corinium Museum. Roman Cirencester was famous for its mosaic artists, who executed mosaics for the villa at Chedworth and other country houses of the local aristocracy.*

Cotswolds

Above *The Rollright Stones north of Chipping Norton in Oxfordshire, a prehistoric stone circle, originally of some 20 stones, 104ft (31m) in diameter. They are known as the King's Men and legend says they were the army of an arrogant king who, with their leader, were turned to stone by a witch. Persistent rumours link this site with witch meetings today.*

Right *House and farmland at Coln St Aldwyns, an attractive village in the Coln Valley. It takes its name from St Aldwyn, a pious Lincolnshire abbot of the 8th century, to whom the church was originally dedicated.*

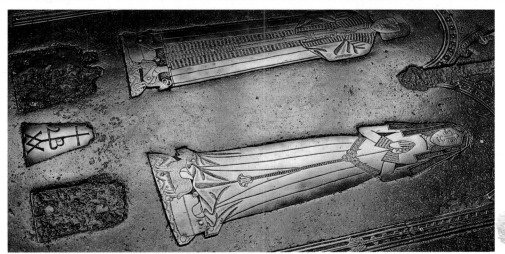

Left *The 15th-century church of St Peter and St Paul at Northleach is one of the finest in the Cotswolds and is known for the brasses of prosperous local wool merchants. This one is to Thomas Busshe and his wife Joan. At their feet are woolsacks.*

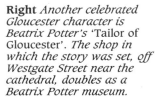

Robert Raikes
Founder of Sunday Schools
Lived Here 1758-1801 Built about 1560

FREE HOUSE

REE HOUSE

Above *In Southgate Street, Gloucester, stands the 16th-century black-and-white house of Robert Raikes, a local worthy who was the leading figure in the development of Sunday schools. He owned the* Gloucester Journal, *which enabled him to publicise the Sunday school he opened in the city in 1780. His house in now a pub.*

Right *Another celebrated Gloucester character is Beatrix Potter's 'Tailor of Gloucester'. The shop in which the story was set, off Westgate Street near the cathedral, doubles as a Beatrix Potter museum.*

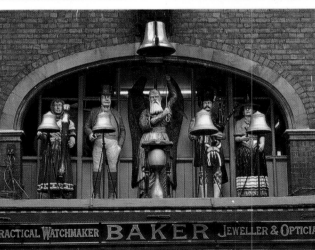

Left *One of Gloucester's curiosities is a clock made in 1904, above a jeweller's in Southgate Street. A veritable mixed bag of figures – Father Time, John Bull, a kilted Scotsman, a Welsh woman and an Irish colleen – strike the hours.*

Above *Scene in Gloucester docks, which were built to serve the 16-mile (25km) canal between the city and Sharpness, opened in 1827 to bypass the treacherous shifting mudbanks of the Severn. The area has now been rescued from decay and is home to a new National Waterways Museum. The successful television serial,* The Onedin Line, *was filmed here.*

Cotswolds

Below *The massive tower of the cathedral, 225ft (68m) high, is seen beyond the garden wall. Ornately pinnacled, it was built in 1450. Only the personal intervention of Oliver Cromwell saved the cathedral from being torn down by Puritan zealots after the Civil War.*

Right *The head of Edward II, from the effigy on the king's tomb in Gloucester Cathedral. Edward's body was brought here after he had been barbarously murdered at Berkeley Castle in 1327. Reports spread of miracles at his tomb, pilgrims flocked to the scene and the income from them paid for the church to be magnificently rebuilt.*

Left *Some of the earliest fan vaulting in the country is in the cathedral cloisters. The rebuilding of the abbey church in the 14th century produced one of the first essays in the New Perpendicular style of architecture. The church became the cathedral of the new diocese of Gloucester in 1540.*

Following spread *Looking across the Thames to the tower and spire of the great 'wool' church of Lechlade. It was rededicated to St Lawrence, a Spanish saint, in compliment to Queen Katherine of Aragon, who owned the manor in the early 16th century. From here eastwards the Thames is navigable for large craft and Cotswold stone was shipped from here for St Paul's and other buildings in London and Oxford.*

Cotswolds

Opposite page *The Cotswold country is known for beautiful gardens and houses. One of the finest gardens was constructed at Hidcote Manor near Chipping Campden by Major Lawrence Johnston, from before World War I to his death in 1958. It is cared for now by the National Trust.*

Right *Topiary birds guard the entrance to the pool garden at Hidcote. The grounds are divided up into separate garden 'rooms' of different character, each with a theme of hue, scent or shape.*

24

Right *Kelmscott Manor, a serene 16th-century house, was William Morris's country retreat until his death in 1896. Now owned by the Society of Antiquaries, the house is occasionally open to the public. Morris is buried in Kelmscott churchyard.*

Above *Seen across Cirencester street market is the church of St John the Baptist, one of the largest parish churches in England, with a handsome tower, 162ft (50m) tall. Beneath it are the carved stone heads of the Earls of Kent and Salisbury, executed in the market place in 1400 for plotting against Henry IV.*

Left *The grand 18th-century house in the background, shielded by a stout yew hedge, is Cirencester Park, seat of Lord Bathurst. Alexander Pope, the poet, advised on the classical design of the noble wooded park behind the mansion. Polo is played here nowadays.*

Cotswolds

Near right *The morning room in Berkeley Castle, with its particularly fine timber roof. The room was formerly a chapel, and the Brussels tapestries are on Old Testament themes. The Berkeley family have lived in this formidable stronghold, guarding the Vale of Berkeley, for more than 800 years.*

Far right *Built of the local red sandstone, Berkeley Castle still has its massive 12th-century keep and bridge over the moat. Edward II was held prisoner here and brutally murdered in 1327. The castle still shows signs of the battering it took from Oliver Cromwell during the Civil War.*

28

Above *One of the attractions at Berkeley Castle today is a butterfly house. Its rough walls mellowed by time, the castle stands among lush Severn meadows where the cattle graze. The family once owned Berkeley Square in London, to which it gave its name.*

Left *Sudeley Castle, near Winchcombe, was the home of Queen Katherine Parr, Henry VIII's last wife, who survived him. She is buried in the chapel, whose tower can be seen among the trees, with a very fine tomb designed by Sir George Gilbert Scott in 1858. The castle was badly damaged during the Civil War and the ruins of the Elizabethan banqueting hall are hauntingly evocative.*

To the Glory of God & in memory of Theodore Emmett of this town who died 13th April 1897 aged 54 and of Mary his wife

Cotswolds

Previous spread *The 19th-century 'Last Supper' stained-glass window in the south aisle of St Mary's Church in Cheltenham is a favourite with visitors. There is much good Victorian glass in the church, which also boasts a fine 14th-century broach spire.*

Above *One of the handsomest Regency towns in the country, Cheltenham owed its initial expansion to the discovery in 1715 of a healing spring. In 1788 George III took his family there for a holiday, which made the town fashionable. With the gardens in the foreground, the stucco terrace houses of Imperial Square are typical of Regency Cheltenham.*

Right *The greengrocery in fashionable Montpellier Walk appropriately has a Regency-striped awning.*

Above *This fountain in the Promenade is a copy of the Trevi Fountain in Rome. The delightful mixture of Regency architecture, tree-lined streets and gardens makes Cheltenham a particularly engaging town.*

Left *The Promenade was originally laid out in 1818 as an avenue of private houses and hotels. By this time Cheltenham's reputation was assured, because the great Duke of Wellington had stayed there to take the waters for his liver. The town became a haven for 'liverish' ex-Indian Army officers and other colonials who retired there for their health.*

Cotswolds

Above *The Cotswold area is rich in imposing country houses. Barrington Park at Great Barrington was built in the 1730s in the Palladian style for Earl Talbot, on a shelf of ground overlooking the River Windrush. The course of the river was diverted to give a better view of it from the house.*

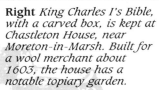

Right *King Charles I's Bible, with a carved box, is kept at Chastleton House, near Moreton-in-Marsh. Built for a wool merchant about 1603, the house has a notable topiary garden.*

Above *The Windrush flows swiftly past the haunting ruins of the 15th-century manor house of the Lovells at Minster Lovell. The family were strong supporters of Richard III and were ruined when he was defeated by Henry VII at Bosworth in 1485. Two years later, the 13th Lord Lovell took refuge here after fighting for the pretender Lambert Simnel, and the tradition is that he starved to death in a locked room in the house.*

Following spread *Houses in the grey local stone at Upper Slaughter, near Stow-on-the-Wold. There is a ford over the River Eye at this typical Cotswold village, whose name has nothing to do with killing, but may be derived from the Old English for 'the place of the pools' or 'of the slough'.*

Above *Life and work in the old days: farm waggons in the Cotswold Countryside Collection at Northleach. This museum of rural life has a substantial array of farm vehicles, agricultural implements and rustic bygones. It is in a former 'house of correction', or combined prison and reformatory, built by one of the local gentry between 1787 and 1791.*

Right *'For Disorders of Horses, Cattle, Sheep and Pigs': inside the lid of a country vet's medicine box, from the Cotswold Countryside Collection, at Northleach, is an advertisement for a Crewe firm of specialists in animal potions and draughts.*

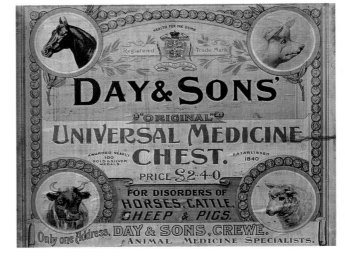

Following spread *The massive 148ft (45m) tower of the abbey church at Tewkesbury dominates the town: the pinnacles were added in 1660. The abbey was immensely rich from the proceeds of sheep and the magnificent church today is still much as it was in the Middle Ages.*

Left *This handsome basketwork wheelchair is in the museum of bygones at Arlington Mill in Bibury. Agricultural and weaving implements are also on display in the 17th-century mill, in this exceptionally pretty village.*

Below *Weaving with machinery of a bygone age in an 18th-century barn at the Cotswold Woollen Weavers in Filkins. This Oxfordshire village has become a haven for craft workshops. The original Cotswolds textile industry was killed by the industrial revolution.*

Cotswolds

Below *Riding in the mill stream at Lower Slaughter, with the waterwheel in the background. The mill chimney in red brick was added early in the 19th century and makes a striking contrast with the Cotswold stone of the rest of the village.*

Right *Sleepy Cotswold villages and hamlets in the warm local stone seem to preserve the tranquil atmosphere of the pre-industrial age. A simple little bridge crosses the Eye at Upper Slaughter. All the village houses are built of stone quarried in the parish.*

Right *Cottages near Bibury. Cotswolds limestone is called oolite, or 'egg stone', because it consists of little round grains like a fish's roe. It can be cut easily when first quarried, but hardens on exposure to the weather, which makes it a valuable building stone.*

Left *Cottages at Lower Slaughter, with the brook in the foreground. The older houses in the village date from around 1600, and most of the cottages are roofed with slates made of Cotswold stone.*

Cotswolds

Below *Roadside cottages and gardens at North Cerney. This Gloucestershire village is in the valley of the River Churn, north of Cirencester. The river flows down to join the Thames at Cricklade. Most of the cottages here were built in the 1600s and 1700s.*

Right *Part of the house and garden of Kiftsgate Court, near Chipping Campden. The garden, which is famous for old-fashioned roses and unusual plants, including tree peonies and abutilons, was created between 1920 and 1950.*

Right *Standing on a knoll with a marvellous view over the River Severn, the church at Oldbury-on-Severn was almost entirely rebuilt in 1899, though the tower is older. It has an extremely unusual dedication, to St Arilda, a local virgin martyr of uncertain date. A local 'tyrant' killed her for refusing to submit to him. Her body was buried in Gloucester Abbey church (now the cathedral), where her shrine was famous for miracles.*

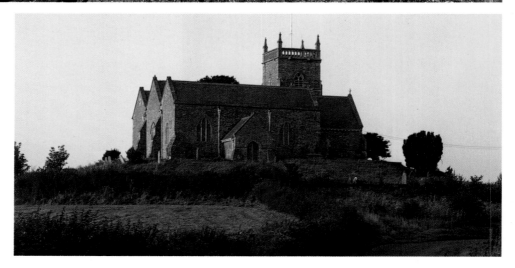

Above *Flowers against grey stone at the post office in Little Barrington. The two Barringtons, Great and Little, stand on either side of the River Windrush, west of Burford. The stone from this area was much in demand, and was used for many of the Oxford colleges and for St Paul's in London.*

46

Left *An enjoyable way of seeing the Cotswold countryside is suggested by the sign of the Air Balloon Inn, outside Birdlip, high on the Cotswold escarpment east of Gloucester. The Cotswold plateau is shaped like a wedge of cheese lying on its side.*

Right *Cottages in a side street in the pleasant town of Winchcombe, down below the steep Cotswold scarp. Mercian kings founded a nunnery and a monastery here, and pilgrims came to the shrine of St Kenelm, a Mercian boy-prince who was murdered by his grasping sister.*

Right *The village of Broadway is one of the showplaces of the Cotswolds, with its cottages and inns, wide main street, two churches and smart shops. Artists and craftsmen from the Pre-Raphaelites onward have been attracted here, including Gordon Russell, who set up his furniture factory in the village.*

Above *A view over the Broadway Tower Country Park, from one of the windows in the tower, a folly designed by James Wyatt in 1794 for the Earl of Coventry. It stands on the steep hill above Broadway village and commands gigantic views.*

Left *Even the ice-cream cart in Broadway's main street is tactfully rigged out in soothing pastel shades. The inn in the background is the Lygon Arms, the village's sumptuous principal hostelry.*

Left *Terraced cottage at Stow-on-the-Wold, 'where the wind blows cold' as the rhyme says. The climbers and shrubs seem to survive well enough, though at 800ft (244m) Stow is the highest town in the Cotswolds. It was once famous for its sheep fair, but today brings flocks of tourists rather than sheep.*

Above 'In summertime on Bredon . . .' *looking out at early morning from Bredon Hill towards the Malverns range to the west. In A E Housman's poem, the lovers* 'see the coloured counties, And hear the larks so high, About us in the sky', *while hearing the church bells ring* 'in valleys miles away'.

Left *Neat cottages and their gardens at Bourton-on-the-Hill, another lofty Cotswold settlement, where the road runs up to the old church of St Lawrence on what was once the main road from London to Worcester.*

Cotswolds

Above *Looking towards Crickley Hill, east of Gloucester on the Cotswolds' edge. The country park and the hill fort on the promontory command splendid views. Archaeologists have found evidence of Stone Age occupation 5000 years ago, but most of what is visible dates from the Iron Age.*

Right *Tending the hanging baskets, while sedulously ignored by the cat, at Blockley, a silk-milling town in the 19th century, between Chipping Campden and Moreton-in-Marsh.*

Left *A ne ne, or Hawaiian goose at the Wildfowl Trust Reserve at Slimbridge, in the marshes where the Berkeley family had their waterfowl preserves. These geese were saved from impending extinction by successful breeding at Slimbridge, and some were sent back to Hawaii to re-establish them in their native haunts.*

Right *'The room of a hundred wheels' at Snowshill Manor. In Gloucestershire, near Broadway, this delightful Tudor manor house contains a remarkable 'magpie museum' of stray objects from penny farthing bicycles and ship models to Japanese armour, camel harness, weavers' tools, clocks and toys, zealously assembled by a former owner, Charles Wade. The collection is presented exactly as he arranged it.*

Below *The house goes back to about 1500, when the manor belonged to Winchcombe Abbey. A later owner was Katherine Parr. It was altered more than once and was restored by Mr Wade at the end of World War I. He gave it to the National Trust in 1951.*

Above *The terraced formal gardens at Snowshill were designed by H Baillie Scott, with old-fashioned roses and shrubs. The village stands high on the Cotswold scarp and straggles down the hill.*

Left *Ann's Room at Snowshill Manor is named after Ann Parsons, a bride who was abducted from Elmley Castle, near Evesham, at dead of night on the eve of St Valentine's Day in 1604 and brought here to be married secretly at midnight.*

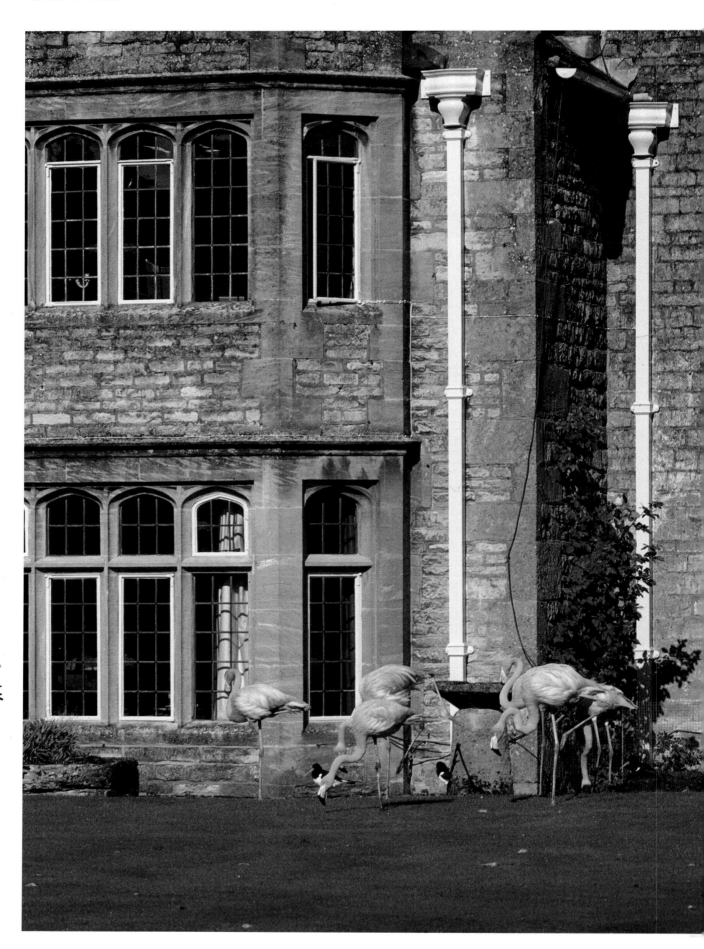

Left *Pink flamingos on the lawn give Chardwar Manor at Bourton-on-the-Water something of an Alice in Wonderland air. The Tudor house is now the home of the Birdland Zoo Garden, with some 600 species of birds.*

Above *Christ with St Mary Magdalene, one of the splendid series of late medieval stained-glass windows in the church of St Mary at Fairford. The church was entirely rebuilt in about 1500 by a rich local wool merchant and his son, and the windows summarise and illustrate the whole Christian faith. They are thought to have been designed by Barnard Flower, Henry VII's master glass painter.*

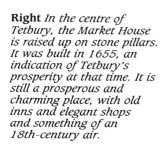

Right *In the centre of Tetbury, the Market House is raised up on stone pillars. It was built in 1655, an indication of Tetbury's prosperity at that time. It is still a prosperous and charming place, with old inns and elegant shops and something of an 18th-century air.*

Above *There are still plenty of sheep on the Cotswolds: view from Cleeve Hill, looking towards the Malvern Hills in the distance. The hill, part of the steep western escarpment, above Winchcombe, is the highest point in the Cotswolds, rising to 1083ft (330m). Cleeve Common is enjoyable open walking country.*

Left *Cottages at Tetbury. It is a hilly town and is known for its gruelling Woolsack Races every year in May, when competitors struggle up a hill with a 1-in-4 gradient carrying 65lb (29¹/₂kg) sacks of wool on their backs.*

Right *A typical view over rolling Cotswold countryside, looking towards Upper Slaughter. The drystone wall in the foreground is characteristic. The fields in this part of England were seldom walled until the 18th century, but today walls like this provide nesting places for robins, wrens and other birds.*

Above *The Norman south doorway of the church of St Peter at Windrush. Built in the 12th century, it has two rows of grotesque pointed beakheads. In the churchyard are some handsome 18th-century table tombs.*

Index

The page numbers in this index refer to the captions and not necessarily to the pictures accompanying them.

Acknowledgements

All the photographs in this publication are from The Automobile Association's photo library, with contributions from:

A Lawson, S Lund, S & O Mathews, E Meacher, R Rainford, R Surman, H Williams and J Wyand with the exception of:
J Beazley 42 Cottages near Bibury, 42/3 Upper Slaughter, 60/1 View over Upper Slaughter; International Photobank Front cover Arlington Row, Bibury; Back cover Upper Slaughter in spring; J Allan Cash Photo Library 28/9 Berkeley Castle.